And So The Journey Begins

Neil J Milliner

Books by Neil J Milliner

BOOKS BY
NEIL J MILLINER

For Jodi DiLiberto— the artist whose vision colors my world.
Your creativity is a reminder that art is not just something we make, but something we live. Your courage, your curiosity, and the way you transform emotion into color continue to inspire every page I write.
To anyone holding this book: If you wish to see the heart behind my own creative life, visit Jodi's work at From the Purple House:
www.fromthepurplehouse.art
Her art is a world of its own—vibrant, intuitive, and deeply human. I'm endlessly grateful to walk beside her.

Contents

DISCLAIMER:

The publisher and the author make no guarantees concerning the level of success you may experience by following the advice and strategies contained in this book, and you accept the risk that results will differ for each individual. The testimonials and examples provided in this book show results, which may not apply to the average reader, and are not intended to represent or guarantee that you will achieve the same or similar results.

The publisher and the author do not make any guarantee or other promise as to any results that may be obtained from using the content of this book. You should never make any investment decision without first consulting with your own financial advisor and conducting your own research and due diligence. To the maximum extent permitted by law, the publisher and the author disclaim any and all liability in the event any information, commentary, analysis, opinions, advice and/or recommendations contained in this book prove to be inaccurate, incomplete or unreliable, or result in any investment or other losses.

Artful Valuation: How Corporate Art Collections Elevate Commercial Property Values

The Hidden Treasures
Within Corporate Walls

Welcome to the world of corporate art collections, where the walls of commercial spaces transform into galleries of inspiration and innovation. In "Artful Valuation," we unravel the often-overlooked connection between corporate art and property values, exploring how a thoughtfully curated collection can elevate the overall worth of commercial real estate.

"The Business of Aesthetics: Crafting an Artful Corporate Identity"

In "The Business of Aesthetics," we delve into the role of art in shaping a distinct corporate identity. Explore how the visual appeal of a well-curated art collection resonates with clients, employees, and investors, creating a unique brand image that contributes to the overall perceived value of the commercial property.

"Beyond the Boardroom: Art as a Productivity and Wellbeing Catalyst"

"Beyond the Boardroom" explores the impact of art on productivity and employee wellbeing. Discover how strategically placed artworks can enhance the work environment, fostering creativity, reducing stress, and contributing to a positive corporate culture. Uncover the correlation between a thriving workforce and increased property value.

"Investing in Inspiration: The Artful

Appeal to Clients and Investors"

"Investing in Inspiration" dives into the ways in which corporate art collections serve as a powerful tool for client engagement and investor attraction. Explore case studies and examples of businesses that have successfully leveraged their art investments to create a captivating narrative, ultimately enhancing the perceived value of their commercial properties.

"Cultural Currency: The Role of Art in Community Engagement"

"Cultural Currency" examines how corporate art collections contribute to community engagement. From public art installations to partnerships with local artists, understand how businesses can become cultural hubs, positively influencing the local community. Explore the link between community connections and heightened property values in the commercial real estate landscape.

"Appraising Art: The Tangible Impact on Property Valuation"

"Appraising Art" takes a closer look at the tangible impact of corporate art collections on property valuation. Explore the methodologies used in appraising art and how these valuations translate into increased property values. Understand the financial significance of investing in art as a long-term strategy for commercial property owners.

"Future-Proofing Investments: Navigating Trends in Corporate Art Collections"

"Future-Proofing Investments" offers insights into navigating trends in corporate art collections. Explore how staying attuned to art market trends and evolving corporate values can ensure that the art investments continue to contribute positively to commercial property values over time. Gain a strategic perspective on aligning art curation with the ever-changing demands of the market.

Less is More: Unveiling the Connection Between Minimalism and Property Value

The Allure of Minimalism in Real Estate

Welcome to the world of minimalism, where simplicity meets sophistication. In "Less is More," we delve into the profound connection between minimalist design and property value. Explore how the principles of minimalism can transform living spaces into timeless havens and elevate the market appeal of your property.

"The Art of Simplification: Understanding Minimalist Design"

In "The Art of Simplification," we unravel the essence of minimalist design. Discover how minimalism goes beyond decluttering and embraces a philosophy that values purposeful and intentional living. Explore the core principles of simplicity, functionality, and the use of negative space that define minimalist aesthetics. Learn how these principles can be applied to various aspects of interior and exterior design to create spaces that exude elegance and timelessness.

Immerse yourself in the art of simplification and understand the fundamentals of minimalist design.

"Decluttered Interiors: Enhancing Space and Market Appeal"

In "Decluttered Interiors," we explore how minimalist interiors contribute to the overall appeal and value of a property. Dive into the concept of decluttered living spaces that promote a sense of tranquility and openness. Understand the strategic use of furniture, color palettes, and lighting to create minimalist interiors that not only feel spacious but also appeal to a broad spectrum of potential buyers. Discover how a clutter-free environment can positively influence the perceived value of a property in the real estate market.

Experience the magic of decluttered interiors and their impact on property marketability and value.

"Curb Appeal in Simplicity: Minimalist Exteriors That Wow"

In "Curb Appeal in Simplicity," we shift our focus to the exterior of properties. Explore how minimalist landscaping and architectural design contribute to the overall curb appeal of a home. Delve into the use of clean lines, natural materials, and a restrained color palette to create exteriors that make a lasting impression. Learn how the minimalist approach to landscaping not only enhances the visual appeal of a property but also requires less maintenance, making it an attractive feature for potential buyers.

Witness the power of curb appeal in simplicity and its influence on property value.

"Timeless Investments: Minimalism and High-End Finishes"

In "Timeless Investments," we discuss the connection between minimalism and high-end finishes. Explore how the use of quality materials and finishes aligns seamlessly with minimalist design principles. Understand the enduring appeal of timeless finishes such as hardwood floors, marble countertops, and stainless-steel appliances in minimalist spaces. Discover how these investments not only enhance the overall aesthetic but also contribute to the long-term value of a property.

Unlock the secrets of timeless investments and their role in the minimalist approach to property value.

"Sustainable Minimalism: Eco-Friendly Practices for Property Value"

In "Sustainable Minimalism," we explore the synergy between minimalism and eco-friendly practices. Understand how the minimalist philosophy aligns with sustainability, promoting a conscious approach to consumption and resource use. Dive into the incorporation of energy-efficient technologies, sustainable materials, and eco-conscious design choices in minimalist homes. Learn how these sustainable practices not only contribute to a healthier planet but also enhance the perceived and actual value of a property in an environmentally conscious market.

Embrace the harmony of sustainable minimalism and its positive impact on property value.

"The Market Appeal of Minimalism: Attracting the Right Buyers"

In "The Market Appeal of Minimalism," we delve into the psychology of buyers and how minimalist design can attract the right audience. Explore how the clean and uncluttered aesthetics of minimalist homes appeal to a broad range of tastes and preferences. Understand the influence of minimalist design on buyer perception, creating an emotional connection that goes beyond visual aesthetics. Discover how positioning your property as a minimalist haven can be a strategic move to stand out in a competitive real estate market.

Uncover the market appeal of minimalism and its role in attracting the right buyers for your property.

Artful Valuation: How Corporate Art Collections Elevate Commercial Property Values

The Hidden Treasures Within Corporate Walls

Welcome to the world of corporate art collections, where the walls of commercial spaces transform into galleries of inspiration and innovation. In "Artful Valuation," we unravel the often-overlooked connection between corporate art and property values, exploring how a thoughtfully curated collection can elevate the overall worth of commercial real estate.

"The Business of Aesthetics: Crafting an Artful Corporate Identity"

In "The Business of Aesthetics," we delve into the role of art in shaping a distinct corporate identity. Explore how the visual appeal of a well-curated art collection resonates with clients, employees, and investors, creating a unique brand image that contributes to the overall perceived value of the commercial property.

"Beyond the Boardroom: Art as a Productivity and Wellbeing Catalyst"

"Beyond the Boardroom" explores the impact of art on productivity and employee wellbeing. Discover how strategically placed artworks can enhance the work environment, fostering creativity, reducing stress, and contributing to a positive corporate culture. Uncover the correlation between a thriving workforce and increased property value.

"Investing in Inspiration: The Artful Appeal to Clients and Investors"

"Investing in Inspiration" dives into the ways in which corporate art collections serve as a powerful tool for client engagement and investor attraction. Explore case studies and examples of businesses that have successfully leveraged their art investments to create a captivating narrative, ultimately enhancing the perceived value of their commercial properties.

"Cultural Currency: The Role of Art in Community Engagement"

"Cultural Currency" examines how corporate art collections contribute to community engagement. From public art installations to partnerships with local artists, understand how businesses can become cultural hubs, positively influencing the local community. Explore the link between community connections and heightened property values in the commercial real estate landscape.

"Appraising Art: The Tangible Impact on Property Valuation"

"Appraising Art" takes a closer look at the tangible impact of corporate art collections on property valuation. Explore the methodologies used in appraising art and how these valuations translate into increased property values. Understand the financial significance of investing in art as a long-term strategy for commercial property owners.

"Future-Proofing Investments: Navigating Trends in Corporate Art Collections"

"Future-Proofing Investments" offers insights into navigating trends in corporate art collections. Explore how staying attuned to art market trends and evolving corporate values can ensure that the art investments continue to contribute positively to commercial property values over time. Gain a strategic perspective on aligning art curation with the ever-changing demands of the market.

Safeguarding Masterpieces: A Comprehensive Guide to Navigating Art Insurance

In the captivating world of art, protecting your investments goes beyond mere brushstrokes and aesthetics. Art insurance emerges as a guardian of your cherished masterpieces, offering a shield against unforeseen circumstances. In this guide, we'll navigate the intricacies of art insurance with a friendly tone, ensuring that you embark on this journey with confidence and clarity.

1: Art Insurance Unveiled: Understanding the Basics

Before delving into the specifics, it's essential to grasp the fundamental principles of art insurance. This section provides a friendly introduction, breaking down the basics of what art insurance is and why it's a crucial component of responsible art ownership. From protecting against theft and damage to considering coverage for transit and storage, understanding the foundational aspects lays the groundwork for a secure art collection.

Transitioning seamlessly from the canvas to the insurance realm, art enthusiasts and collectors alike will find this section a valuable starting point in demystifying the world of art insurance.

2: Appraisal Adventures: Determining the Value of Your Art

The first step in securing art insurance is understanding the value of your collection. This section guides you through the appraisal process, demystifying the intricacies of determining the worth of your artworks. Friendly tips on working with professional appraisers, keeping accurate records, and staying informed about market trends ensure that you embark on your appraisal adventure armed with knowledge and confidence.

Just as an artist carefully crafts each stroke, meticulous attention to detail in the appraisal process sets the stage for comprehensive and accurate art insurance coverage.

3: Tailoring Coverage: Customizing Insurance to Your Collection

Every art collection is as unique as the individual pieces it comprises. This section explores the art of tailoring insurance coverage to suit the specific needs of your collection. From considering the type of art you own to understanding the nuances of different insurance policies, we delve into the friendly intricacies of customizing coverage.

Navigating the insurance landscape becomes an empowering experience as you learn to ask the right questions, ensuring that your coverage aligns with the distinctive character of your art investments.

4: The Quest for the Right Insurer: Choosing Your Art Insurance Partner

Much like selecting the perfect frame for a painting, choosing the right insurer is a critical decision in the art insurance journey. This section provides a friendly guide to the quest for the ideal insurance partner, offering tips on researching reputable insurers, understanding policy terms, and evaluating customer reviews.

With a friendly tone, we navigate the landscape of insurance providers, empowering you to make an informed decision that aligns seamlessly with your art protection needs.

5: Art in Transit: Safeguarding Your Collection on the Move

Whether you're transporting artworks to exhibitions, galleries, or a new home, safeguarding your collection in transit is paramount. This section explores the friendly art of ensuring comprehensive coverage during transportation. From understanding the risks associated with transit to exploring insurance options specifically tailored for art on the move, we guide you through the intricacies of safeguarding your masterpieces on their journey.

Transitioning seamlessly from the stationary gallery to the mobile canvas, this section ensures that your art remains protected and cherished, even when on the move.

6: The Claim Chronicles: Navigating the Art Insurance Claim Process

In the unfortunate event that you need to make a claim, navigating the process with ease is essential. This section offers a friendly guide to the claim chronicles, walking you through the steps of filing a claim, documenting damage, and liaising with your insurer. Understanding the claim process ensures that, in times of adversity, you can navigate the journey with confidence and efficiency. Just as an artist learns from experience, this section empowers you with the knowledge to confidently navigate the claim process, turning potential challenges into manageable steps toward restoration and recovery.

Canvas Capital: Artistic Trends in Real Estate - A Valuable Investment Strategy

The Brushstroke of Value in Real Estate

Welcome to the world where canvas meets capital, exploring the integration of artistic trends as a powerful investment strategy in real estate. In this guide, we unravel the secrets of leveraging art to enhance property value, offering insights into how embracing artistic trends can be a game-changer in the realm of real estate investment. Get ready to embark on a journey where aesthetics and assets seamlessly converge.

"Artful Architecture: The Impact of Art-Inspired Design on Property Value"

In "Artful Architecture," we delve into the impact of art-inspired design on property value. Explore how real estate developers and architects are incorporating artistic elements into their designs, creating visually stunning and unique properties. From avant-garde structures to buildings that mimic famous artworks, discover how artful architecture not only attracts attention but also elevates the perceived value of a property, making it a standout investment in a competitive market.

Witness the transformative power of artful architecture and its influence on the valuation of real estate.

"Curating Value: The Role of Curated Art Collections in Property Enhancement"

In "Curating Value," we explore the rising trend of curated art collections within real estate spaces. Dive into the world of developers strategically curating art pieces to enhance the ambiance and allure of residential and commercial properties. Learn how a well-curated art collection can create a sense of exclusivity, turning a property into a unique investment opportunity. Discover the symbiotic relationship between curated art and property value, where aesthetics drive desirability and, in turn, enhance the investment potential.

Explore the art of curating value and witness how art collections contribute to the overall appeal of real estate.

"Smart Art Integration: The Intersection of Technology and Real Estate Investment"

In "Smart Art Integration," we explore the intersection of technology and real estate investment. Learn how developers are incorporating smart art installations to create immersive and interactive experiences within properties. Dive into the world of digital art, augmented reality, and smart home features that not only provide a modern and luxurious living experience but also contribute to the long-term value of a property. Discover how the marriage of art and technology is shaping the future of real estate investments.

Uncover the possibilities of smart art integration and its impact on the tech-savvy real estate market.

"Artful Neighborhoods: Community Development and Property Values"

In "Artful Neighborhoods," we shift our focus to community development and its impact on property values. Explore how the integration of public art, cultural spaces, and community art initiatives can turn neighborhoods into desirable locations for real estate investment. Learn how the creation of artful communities not only enhances the quality of life for residents but also contributes to the appreciation of property values over time. Discover the ripple effect of artistic engagement on the overall appeal of a neighborhood and its real estate market.

Experience the transformative influence of artful neighborhoods and their role in shaping property values.

"The Art Investor's Dilemma: Navigating Trends for Long-Term Value"

In "The Art Investor's Dilemma," we navigate the complexities of art trends and their impact on long-term property value. Explore the delicate balance between embracing current artistic trends and ensuring enduring value in real estate investments. Learn how to navigate the evolving landscape of artistic preferences, understanding the fine line between trendy and timeless. Gain insights into making informed decisions as an art-focused real estate investor, maximizing the potential for sustained property appreciation.

Confront the art investor's dilemma and discover strategies for long-term value in the dynamic real estate market.

"Art-Infused ROI: The Financial Benefits of Investing in Artistic Real Estate"

In "Art-Infused ROI," we delve into the financial benefits of investing in artistic real estate. Explore case studies and success stories where artful investments have resulted in substantial returns. From increased property values to enhanced rental yields, discover the tangible financial advantages of integrating artistic elements into real estate portfolios. Uncover the potential for art-infused ROI and how strategic investments in creative spaces can yield both aesthetic and financial dividends.

Unlock the secrets of art-infused ROI and witness the financial benefits of investing in artistic real estate.

Artistic Lighting: Illuminating Your Property's Value

Shedding Light on the Art of Illumination

"Artistic Lighting: Illuminating Your Property's Value" unveils the transformative power of lighting as a strategic element in enhancing your property's aesthetic appeal and overall value. Join us on a radiant journey through creative lighting solutions that go beyond functionality to create an artful ambiance.

"The Luminous Landscape: Crafting Ambiance with Outdoor Lighting"

In "The Luminous Landscape," explore the world of outdoor lighting and its profound impact on your property's curb appeal. From pathway lanterns to tree uplighting, discover how carefully designed outdoor lighting can turn your garden into a mesmerizing nighttime oasis, adding both beauty and value to your property.

"Statement Fixtures: Lighting as Sculptural Art"

Delve into the concept of "Statement Fixtures," where lighting becomes more than just a practical necessity. Uncover how sculptural light fixtures can serve as focal points, transforming living spaces into curated galleries. From elegant chandeliers to avant-garde pendant lights, learn how lighting choices can redefine the artistic character of your home.

"Dynamic Color Play: Illuminating Your

Mood with Smart Lighting"

Explore the interactive world of "Dynamic Color Play," where smart lighting takes center stage. Understand how programmable LED lights can be used to create versatile atmospheres, adapting to different occasions and moods. Dive into the possibilities of transforming your living spaces with a simple touch, adding an artistic and dynamic dimension to your property.

"Architectural Accents: Illuminating Unique Property Features"

In "Architectural Accents," discover how lighting can be used to highlight and accentuate the unique features of your property. Whether it's illuminating intricate architectural details, showcasing textured walls, or emphasizing specific design elements, strategic lighting can draw attention to the property's distinctive character, enhancing its overall value.

"Artful Task Lighting: Combining Functionality with Aesthetics"

Uncover the harmony between functionality and aesthetics in "Artful Task Lighting." Explore how task lighting, typically associated with practicality, can be transformed into an artistic expression. From kitchen islands to study nooks, understand how carefully selected task lighting can enhance both functionality and visual appeal.

"Eco-Friendly Illumination: Sustainable Lighting for Modern Homes"

Conclude our exploration with "Eco-Friendly Illumination," where we shed light on sustainable lighting choices. Learn how energy-efficient fixtures, LED technologies, and solar-powered options not only contribute to a greener environment but also elevate the eco-friendly profile of your property, adding a unique dimension to its overall value.

Artful Accents: Drawing Attention to Your Property's Best Features

Setting the Stage with Artful Elegance

Step into a world where art becomes the star of the show, transforming your property into a captivating masterpiece. In "Artful Accents," we explore the transformative power of art as a focal point, guiding you through the process of drawing attention to your property's most exquisite features.

"The Power of First Impressions: Art at the Entryway"

In "The Power of First Impressions," we uncover the art of making a statement right from the entrance. Discover how strategically placed artworks, whether bold sculptures or vibrant installations, can create an immediate and lasting impression, setting the tone for the entire property. Explore the interplay between art and curb appeal as a dynamic duo that captures attention.

"Architectural Harmony: Integrating Art with Design"

"Architectural Harmony" explores the seamless integration of art with your property's design. Dive into the world of art that complements architectural elements, enhancing the overall aesthetic appeal. From sculptures echoing the property's lines to murals that breathe life into empty spaces, discover how art becomes an intrinsic part of your property's design narrative.

"Outdoor Elegance: Sculpting Nature with Art"

"Outdoor Elegance" takes the spotlight to the great outdoors, exploring how art can accentuate the natural beauty of your property. Delve into the world of outdoor sculptures, garden installations, and artistic landscaping that not only draw attention but create a harmonious dialogue with nature, elevating your property's allure.

"Artful Interiors: Enhancing Key Living Spaces"

"Artful Interiors" delves into the heart of your property, exploring how art can enhance key living spaces. From living rooms to dining areas, understand the art of choosing pieces that not only complement the room's function but also draw attention to architectural highlights. Discover how curated art selections can elevate the living experience for residents and guests alike.

"A View to Remember: Art and Scenic Vistas"

"A View to Remember" shifts the focus to properties with scenic vistas, exploring how art can enhance these breathtaking backdrops. Whether overlooking city skylines, mountains, or oceans, learn how to strategically position art to frame and complement these natural panoramas. Uncover the secrets to creating picturesque views that become iconic features of your property.

"Investing in Artful Value: The Impact on Property Appreciation"

"Investing in Artful Value" concludes our exploration, delving into the impact of art on property appreciation. Understand how the careful curation of art can contribute to the long-term value of your property. From attracting potential buyers to creating a distinct brand for your property, discover the financial and aesthetic rewards of making art a focal point.

The Influence of Art in Real Estate Photography: Online Presence Matters

Framing Success - The Art of Real Estate Photography

"Online Presence Matters: The Influence of Art in Real Estate Photography" uncovers the pivotal role artistic photography plays in shaping the digital narrative of your property. Join us as we explore the transformative impact of captivating visuals on potential buyers and delve into the strategies that turn online browsers into offline visitors.

"The Art of First Impressions: Capturing Attention with Stunning Visuals"

In "The Art of First Impressions," we explore the idea that a picture is worth a thousand words. Understand how high-quality, artfully composed images act as the first handshake between your property and prospective buyers, setting the tone for a positive and memorable experience.

"Beyond Point-and-Shoot: The Photographer as an Artist"

Delve into the world of skilled photographers in "Beyond Point-and-Shoot." Uncover the artistry involved in capturing the essence of a property, from understanding lighting and angles to post-processing techniques that enhance visual appeal. Discover how the photographer's artistic touch transforms ordinary spaces into compelling narratives.

"Styling and Staging: Crafting Visual Stories That Sell"

Explore the collaborative dance of "Styling and Staging." Understand how a skilled photographer works hand-in-hand with stylists and stagers to create visually engaging stories. Learn how the careful arrangement of furniture, decor, and lighting can turn an empty room into a warm, inviting space that resonates with potential buyers.

"Emotional Connection Through Visual Storytelling"

In "Emotional Connection Through Visual Storytelling," we discuss the power of creating an emotional bond through photography. Explore how artful compositions can evoke emotions, helping potential buyers envision themselves living in the space. Uncover the psychology behind visual storytelling and its impact on the decision-making process.

"The Virtual Tour Experience: Navigating Through Artful Narratives"

Embark on a virtual journey in "The Virtual Tour Experience." Understand how technology has elevated real estate photography beyond static images, offering immersive virtual tours. Explore the art of creating seamless narratives that guide potential buyers through a property, creating an interactive and engaging experience.

"Optimizing Online Presence: Social Media, Websites, and Beyond"

Conclude our exploration with "Optimizing Online Presence." Delve into the strategies for leveraging social media platforms, real estate websites, and other digital channels to maximize the impact of your visually compelling content. Learn how a strong online presence can drive engagement, generate leads, and ultimately turn clicks into property visits.

Green Gallery: Eco-Friendly Wall Art Options for Sustainable Property Value

Sustainably Shaping Spaces with Eco-Friendly Wall Art

Welcome to the future of interior design where sustainability meets aesthetics. In "Green Gallery," we explore the diverse realm of eco-friendly wall art options that not only enhance the visual appeal of spaces but also contribute to sustainable property value. Join us on a journey through innovative and environmentally conscious art choices that make a positive impact on both your living space and the planet.

"Nature's Palette: Botanical Wall Art for Biophilic Bliss"

In "Nature's Palette," we dive into the world of botanical wall art, celebrating the beauty of nature within your living spaces. Explore the serene allure of botanical prints, moss walls, and sustainably sourced wooden art that brings the outdoors inside. Discover how these eco-friendly options not only enhance the aesthetics of a property but also foster a sense of well-being and connection to nature, creating a harmonious environment that can positively influence property values.

Immerse yourself in the calming embrace of nature's palette and its impact on sustainable property value.

"Recycled Revelry: Artistic Creations from Upcycled Materials"

In "Recycled Revelry," we unravel the artistic possibilities of upcycled materials, turning discarded items into stunning pieces of wall art. Explore how artists and designers are creatively repurposing materials like reclaimed wood, metal, and plastics to craft unique and eco-friendly art installations. Delve into the world of sustainable sculptures and wall hangings that not only tell a story of renewal but also contribute to a circular economy, adding an element of conscious creativity to your property.

Witness the magic of recycled revelry and how upcycled art can be a sustainable asset for your living spaces.

"Solar-Powered Statements: Harnessing Energy for Artistic Illumination"

In "Solar-Powered Statements," we explore the integration of solar technology into wall art, transforming your space into a beacon of sustainable design. Discover the artful possibilities of solar-powered LED installations, creating dynamic and energy-efficient statements that illuminate your property. Learn how these eco-friendly options not only reduce energy consumption but also add a futuristic and visually striking element to your walls, enhancing both the aesthetic and sustainable appeal of your living space.

Experience the brilliance of solar-powered statements and their impact on sustainable property value.

"Canvas and Cork: Sustainable Materials for Artistic Expression"

In "Canvas and Cork," we shift our focus to sustainable materials that redefine artistic expression. Explore the versatility of cork as a canvas for eco-friendly wall art, offering not only a unique texture but also sustainable harvesting practices. Dive into the world of corkboard murals, paintings, and wall coverings that contribute to a healthier indoor environment while making a positive statement about your commitment to sustainable living. Uncover the artistry of canvas and cork and how these materials are elevating the green quotient of modern interiors.

Embrace the sustainable elegance of canvas and cork and witness their transformative impact on property value.

"Living Walls: Verdant Vertical Gardens for Sustainable Luxury"

In "Living Walls," we embark on a journey into the realm of verdant vertical gardens, turning walls into lush, sustainable masterpieces. Explore the beauty of living art installations that incorporate real plants and moss, not only purifying the air but also creating a refreshing and vibrant atmosphere. Learn how living walls contribute to sustainability by improving indoor air quality and providing insulation, making them a unique and impactful addition to any property seeking a touch of green luxury.

Immerse yourself in the sustainable opulence of living walls and their contribution to property value.

"Eco-Conscious Investments: The Long-Term Impact of Sustainable Wall Art"

In "Eco-Conscious Investments," we discuss the long-term impact of sustainable wall art on property value. Understand how eco-friendly choices can contribute to a property's desirability and market appeal. Explore case studies highlighting the financial benefits of sustainable investments, from increased energy efficiency to a positive perception among eco-conscious buyers. Gain insights into the growing demand for sustainable features in real estate and how embracing eco-friendly wall art can position your property as a forward-thinking and valuable investment.

Unlock the secrets of eco-conscious investments and witness the lasting impact on sustainable property value.

The Impact of Wall Art on Property Value: A Comprehensive Guide

Brushing Up on Home Aesthetics

Welcome to a journey through the interplay of aesthetics and property value in our guide on "The Impact of Wall Art on Property Value." In this comprehensive exploration, we'll delve into the transformative power of wall art, unraveling how a stroke of a brush or a carefully chosen piece can significantly influence the perceived and actual value of a property. From curb appeal to interior design, discover how art becomes an unsung hero in the real estate arena.

Curb Appeal Chronicles - The First Impression

Embark on "Curb Appeal Chronicles," where we investigate the pivotal role of exterior wall art in shaping the first impressions of potential buyers. This section explores how a well-designed mural, tasteful sculptures, or artistic fencing can enhance the visual appeal of a property, making it stand out in a competitive market. Dive into the psychology behind curb appeal and learn how the right art choices can elevate the perceived value of a home before the front door is even opened.

Investing in curb appeal isn't just about attracting potential buyers; it's about creating a welcoming atmosphere that resonates with the neighborhood. By strategically incorporating wall art into the exterior design, homeowners can contribute to the overall aesthetics of the community, positively impacting property values for everyone.

Interior Elegance - Art as a Key Player in Home Design

Step into "Interior Elegance," where we explore the profound impact of wall art on the interior design of homes. This section delves into the way carefully chosen pieces can elevate the ambiance, creating a sense of luxury and sophistication. From classic paintings to modern installations, discover how the right art can turn a house into a personalized haven, affecting not only the homeowners' enjoyment but also the perceived value for potential buyers.

The transformative power of interior elegance lies in its ability to create a cohesive and visually pleasing environment. Homebuyers are not just looking for a place to live; they are searching for a lifestyle. By integrating art into the interior design, homeowners can communicate a unique narrative that resonates with potential buyers, ultimately impacting the property's value.

Investment Insights - Art as a Tangible Asset

Explore "Investment Insights," where we unravel the concept of art as a tangible asset that contributes to the overall value of a property. This section discusses the potential appreciation of art over time and how savvy homeowners can make strategic art investments to boost the financial worth of their homes. Dive into the world of art valuation, understanding how certain pieces can become not just decorative elements but valuable assets.

The transformative power of investment insights lies in its ability to position art as more than mere decoration; it becomes a strategic financial move. Homeowners can explore the world of art collection, not only for personal enjoyment but also as a way to enhance the long-term value of their properties, creating a unique intersection of aesthetics and financial acumen.

Cultural Connection – The Influence of Local Art Scenes

Step into "Cultural Connection," where we examine the impact of connecting a property to the local art scene. This section delves into how homeowners can contribute to the cultural identity of their community by showcasing local artists or embracing regional art styles. Uncover how this cultural connection can create a sense of belonging, making a property more appealing to buyers who appreciate the richness of the local creative scene.

The transformative power of cultural connection lies in its ability to turn a property into a canvas that reflects the soul of its surroundings. By integrating local art into the home, homeowners not only support the local creative community but also tap into a unique selling point that can significantly influence the perceived and actual value of their property.

Expressive Exteriors – The Rise of Outdoor Art Installations

Embark on "Expressive Exteriors," where we explore the growing trend of incorporating outdoor art installations into property design. This section delves into the impact of sculptures, murals, and other outdoor artworks on the overall appeal of a property. Discover how these expressive exteriors contribute to creating immersive living spaces that extend beyond the confines of the four walls.

The transformative power of expressive exteriors lies in their ability to blur the lines between indoor and outdoor living. Homeowners can create enchanting outdoor spaces that not only enhance their own quality of life but also make a lasting impression on potential buyers, influencing the perceived value of the property as a harmonious blend of nature and art.

Future Frontiers - Art and Smart Home Integration

Conclude our exploration with "Future Frontiers," where we delve into the intersection of art and smart home integration. This section investigates how technology-driven art installations and digital displays can be seamlessly incorporated into modern homes, creating dynamic, ever-changing visual experiences. Discover the potential of these futuristic integrations to not only enhance the aesthetics of a property but also appeal to tech-savvy buyers.

The transformative power of future frontiers lies in its ability to position homes at the forefront of innovation. As technology becomes an integral part of daily life, homeowners can leverage artful smart home integrations to not only elevate their living spaces but also future-proof their properties, influencing the perceived and actual value in the ever-evolving real estate landscape.

Art Beyond Aesthetics: Unveiling the Connection Between Wall Art and Home Appraisal

The Unseen Value of Wall Art

Welcome to "Art Beyond Aesthetics," where we delve into the intricate relationship between wall art and home appraisal. In this enlightening journey, we'll uncover how the pieces that adorn your walls aren't just expressions of your style but can significantly impact the perceived and actual value of your home. Let's explore the fascinating interplay of art and appraisal, unraveling the ways in which your cherished wall decor goes beyond aesthetics to become an integral part of your property's worth.

"Curation Elevation: Setting the Scene for Value"

In "Curation Elevation," we dive into the art of selection and curation, exploring how a well-chosen collection can set the scene for increased home value. Discover the psychology behind selecting pieces that resonate with potential buyers and appraisers alike. From thematic coherence to the strategic placement of art, learn how to craft a narrative that enhances the overall appeal of your home, contributing to a positive impression that transcends the visual.

Curation elevation isn't just about aesthetics; it's about creating a curated experience that speaks to the hearts of those who enter your home. Uncover the secrets of choosing art that elevates not only your living space but also the perceived value of your property.

"The Art of Perception: Influencing Buyer Impressions"

In "The Art of Perception," we unravel the subtle ways in which wall art shapes the perception of potential buyers. Explore the psychological impact of art on mood, atmosphere, and the overall feel of a space. From the bold strokes of contemporary pieces to the timeless charm of classical works, understand how different styles can evoke emotions that contribute to a positive buyer impression. Dive into the artful details that can make your home memorable and desirable, ultimately influencing its perceived value.

The art of perception isn't just about visual appeal; it's about creating an emotional connection that resonates with those looking for their next home. Explore the nuances of buyer psychology and discover how your wall art can play a crucial role in influencing their perceptions and decisions.

"Beyond the Canvas: Art as Home Integration"

In "Beyond the Canvas," we explore how art seamlessly integrated into the architecture and design of your home contributes to its overall value. Investigate how murals, bespoke installations, and purposeful design can become valuable assets that appraisers consider when evaluating your property. From accentuating architectural features to creating a sense of unity, learn how the integration of art goes beyond mere decoration, becoming an essential component of your home's appraisal worth.

Beyond the canvas isn't just about adornment; it's about fostering a sense of integration and cohesion that enhances the intrinsic value of your property. Discover how purposeful design and artistic integration can become valuable contributors to your home's appraisal.

"Investment Art: Valuable Additions to Your Home Equity"

In "Investment Art," we explore the concept of art as an investment that appreciates over time, adding tangible value to your home equity. Delve into the world of collecting pieces that go beyond personal taste and serve as valuable assets in the eyes of appraisers. Understand how strategic art acquisitions can yield returns, making your home not just a living space but a wise investment that stands the test of time.

Investment art isn't just about aesthetics; it's about acquiring pieces that appreciate in value, contributing to the overall financial worth of your property. Explore the possibilities of turning your art collection into a powerful component of your home equity.

"Art in the Details: Small Pieces, Big Impact"

In "Art in the Details," we celebrate the often-overlooked impact of small pieces and intricate details on the perceived and appraised value of your home. Explore how carefully chosen sculptures, framed photographs, or unique artifacts can add character and charm, subtly influencing appraisers and potential buyers. Learn how to use the details to tell a compelling story about your home, elevating its worth beyond the square footage and basic features.

Art in the details isn't just about size; it's about recognizing the potential for big impacts in the smallest corners of your home. Uncover the secrets of using intricate details to create a lasting impression that transcends the expected and contributes to the overall value of your property.

"Appraising the Unseen: Quantifying the Value of Art"

Conclude our exploration in "Appraising the Unseen," where we demystify the often-intangible value that art brings to your home. Delve into the methodologies appraisers use to quantify the impact of art on the overall value of a property. Understand the metrics and considerations that go beyond aesthetics, shedding light on the complex yet fascinating process of appraising the unseen but deeply felt value that your wall art brings to your home.

Appraising the unseen isn't just about numbers; it's about understanding the nuanced process that appraisers undertake to assess the impact of art on your property's overall worth. Gain insights into the appraisal methodology and the considerations that transform your cherished pieces into quantifiable assets.

Navigating the Digital Canvas: A Friendly Guide to Successful Online Art Purchases

In the vibrant world of online art buying, the digital canvas is your gateway to a myriad of creative treasures. This friendly guide offers tips and insights to ensure that your online art purchase is not just a transaction but a delightful journey into the realm of artistic discovery.

The Art of Browsing: Navigating Online Galleries with Finesse

Browsing through online galleries is like strolling through a virtual art fair, and the art of navigating these digital spaces requires finesse. This section provides friendly tips on refining your search, utilizing filters effectively, and exploring curated collections. By honing your browsing skills, you can unearth hidden gems that align with your artistic preferences and add a personal touch to your collection.

Transitioning seamlessly between genres and styles, this section encourages art enthusiasts to embrace the adventure of discovery, allowing the digital canvas to unfold a myriad of artistic possibilities.

Beyond Pixels: Understanding Art Descriptions and Details

When buying art online, the screen becomes your portal to creativity, but understanding the details is crucial. This section guides you through the importance of reading art descriptions, understanding dimensions, and paying attention to framing details. Friendly insights on deciphering artistic intent, medium specifics, and the story behind each piece ensure that you make informed choices that resonate with your artistic sensibilities.

Just as a magnifying glass reveals intricate details in a painting, this section empowers you to go beyond pixels, appreciating the nuances that make each artwork unique. The journey into understanding art details transforms online browsing into a curated experience.

Virtual Viewing Rooms: Embracing the Online Exhibition Experience

Online art platforms often offer virtual viewing rooms, providing a simulated gallery experience from the comfort of your space. This section explores the friendly dynamics of embracing virtual exhibitions, offering tips on navigating 3D spaces, attending online openings, and interacting with artworks in a digital setting. By immersing yourself in these virtual environments, you not only preview the scale and context of artworks but also gain a sense of the artist's intended presentation.

Transitioning seamlessly from one virtual room to another, this section encourages art enthusiasts to savor the digital exhibition experience, transforming online art buying into a dynamic and interactive journey.

Connecting with Artists: The Art of Virtual Studio Visits

In the online art world, connecting with artists is not limited to physical studio visits; virtual encounters provide unique opportunities for engagement. This section guides you through the art of virtual studio visits, offering tips on participating in artist talks, following artists on social media, and exploring behind-the-scenes content. By establishing a connection with artists, you not only gain insights into their creative process but also contribute to a more personalized and meaningful art-buying experience.

Just as a face-to-face conversation with an artist adds depth to your understanding of their work, this section encourages art enthusiasts to embrace the digital dialogue, fostering connections that go beyond the confines of the online platform.

Secure Transactions: Ensuring a Safe and Trustworthy Purchase

Ensuring secure transactions is paramount when buying art online. This section provides friendly advice on verifying the legitimacy of online platforms, understanding payment options, and confirming shipping and return policies. By prioritizing secure transactions, you can approach online art buying with confidence, knowing that your purchases are protected, and your investment is in safe hands.

Navigating the digital payment landscape with ease, this section encourages art enthusiasts to focus on the joy of acquiring art, free from concerns about the security of their transactions.

Unboxing the Experience: Reveling in the Arrival of Your Art

The climax of the online art buying journey is the arrival of your chosen piece. This section offers tips on unboxing your art, inspecting it for any damage, and celebrating the moment. Friendly insights on creating a dedicated space for your new acquisition and sharing the unboxing experience with the artist and the online community add a touch of communal joy to your art-buying adventure.

As you unwrap your carefully packaged artwork, this section invites you to revel in the tangible experience, transforming the digital transaction into a memorable and delightful moment of artistic connection.

Home Sweet SOLD: Unleashing the Magic of Statement Wall Art in Your Home Sale

The Art of Home Selling

Welcome to "Home Sweet SOLD," where we uncover the transformative power of statement wall art in the realm of home selling. In this journey, we'll explore how a carefully curated collection of impactful pieces can be the secret weapon in making your home stand out in a crowded market. Join us as we delve into the nuances of statement wall art and discover how it can turn your property from a listing into a buyer's dream.

"Curb Appeal Redefined: The Impact of Exterior Art"

In "Curb Appeal Redefined," we break the mold by exploring the often-underestimated impact of exterior wall art on the first impression of your home. Dive into the world of eye-catching murals, vibrant sculptures, and tasteful installations that can instantly elevate your home's curb appeal. Learn how the right exterior art sets the stage for a positive walkthrough experience, enticing potential buyers from the moment they set eyes on your property.

Curb Appeal Redefined isn't just about what's inside; it's about creating an allure that starts at the front door. Discover the secrets to making a lasting impression, beginning with the unique and captivating statement art that adorns your home's exterior.

"Welcoming Statements: Foyers and Entryways That Wow"

In "Welcoming Statements," we move beyond the front door to explore how statement wall art in foyers and entryways can set the tone for the entire home tour. Delve into the art of making a grand entrance, whether it's through bold paintings, captivating sculptures, or thoughtfully arranged gallery walls. Understand the psychology behind creating a welcoming atmosphere that draws buyers into the heart of your home, making a lasting impression from the moment they step inside.

Welcoming Statements aren't just about aesthetics; they're about creating an emotional connection. Discover how strategically placed statement art in entryways can make potential buyers feel instantly at home, setting the stage for a memorable and positive viewing experience.

"Living Large: Transforming Living Spaces with Statement Art"

In "Living Large," we unravel the secrets of turning your living spaces into captivating showcases through the power of statement wall art. Explore the impact of oversized paintings, distinctive sculptures, and bold installations in living rooms, creating an environment that sparks the imagination of potential buyers. Learn how to use statement art to accentuate architectural features, highlight key selling points, and foster a sense of luxury and sophistication that resonates with those seeking their dream home.

Living Large isn't just about size; it's about making a bold statement that leaves a lasting impression. Discover how to transform your living spaces into visually stunning masterpieces that captivate the senses and make your home a standout in the competitive real estate market.

"Dining in Style: Elevating the Dining Experience with Art"

In "Dining in Style," we explore the often-overlooked potential of statement wall art in dining areas. From unique installations to carefully chosen pieces that complement the dining ambiance, discover how art can elevate the overall dining experience for potential buyers. Uncover the secrets to creating a sophisticated and inviting space that invites imagination and sparks conversation, turning every meal into a memorable event.

Dining in Style isn't just about functionality; it's about creating an immersive experience. Learn how to make your dining areas unforgettable, adding an extra layer of appeal that resonates with buyers looking for a home that goes beyond the basics.

"The Bedroom Retreat: Statement Art for Relaxation and Luxury"

In "The Bedroom Retreat," we delve into the private sanctuary of your home, exploring how statement art can transform bedrooms into luxurious retreats. From serene paintings to unique headboard installations, understand the art of creating a calming and inviting atmosphere that resonates with potential buyers seeking a tranquil haven. Discover how to strike the perfect balance between personal expression and universal appeal, making your bedrooms irresistible to those envisioning their dream home.

The Bedroom Retreat isn't just about aesthetics; it's about creating a space that speaks to the emotions and desires of potential buyers. Learn how to turn your bedrooms into showcases of comfort and style, leaving a lasting impression that goes beyond the surface.

"Artful Investments: Maximizing Returns with Statement Pieces"

In "Artful Investments," we shift the focus to the potential returns on investment that come with strategically incorporating statement wall art into your home selling strategy. Explore the psychology behind buyer decisions and understand how a carefully curated collection can enhance your property's perceived value. From creating a competitive edge in the market to justifying a higher asking price, discover the art of turning your collection into a valuable asset in the sales process.

Artful Investments aren't just about aesthetics; they're about leveraging the power of statement art to maximize the returns on your home sale. Uncover the secrets of making artful choices that translate into a higher perceived and actual value for your property.

Wall Art in Vacation Homes: Elevating the Rental Property Experience

Artful Escapes - The Power of Wall Decor in Vacation Rentals

Embark on a journey with "Wall Art in Vacation Homes: Elevating the Rental Property Experience" as we explore how thoughtfully curated wall art can transform a temporary dwelling into a memorable escape. Discover the nuances of creating an artful ambiance that enchants guests and keeps them coming back for more.

"The Welcome Canvas: First Impressions Matter"

In "The Welcome Canvas," uncover the significance of creating a captivating first impression through carefully chosen wall art. Delve into the psychology of guest expectations and learn how strategically placed artwork sets the stage for a delightful vacation experience from the moment they step through the door.

"Local Flavor on Display: Connecting Guests with the Destination"

Explore the concept of "Local Flavor on Display," where we discuss the artful integration of local artwork to create a sense of place. Discover how showcasing regional artists or incorporating elements of the destination's culture through wall decor enhances the overall guest experience, fostering a connection between visitors and the locale.

"Creating Ambiance: The Art of Theme-Based Decor"

In "Creating Ambiance," we unravel the art of theme-based decor that transforms vacation homes into thematic retreats. Learn how selecting wall art that complements the overall design theme - whether it be coastal, rustic, or contemporary - contributes to a cohesive and immersive atmosphere that resonates with guests.

"Art for Comfort: Making Spaces Feel Like Home"

Delve into "Art for Comfort" as we explore how well-chosen wall art contributes to the homely feel of vacation rentals. Discover the subtle ways in which artwork can enhance comfort, creating a welcoming environment that encourages relaxation and allows guests to fully unwind during their stay.

"Insta-Worthy Spaces: The Social Media Influence of Artful Interiors"

Uncover the significance of "Insta-Worthy Spaces" and the impact of visually appealing interiors on social media engagement. Explore how vacation homes adorned with eye-catching wall art become shareable havens, attracting attention on social platforms, and generating organic marketing for property owners.

"Practical Considerations: Durability, Maintenance, and Flexibility"

Conclude our journey with "Practical Considerations," addressing the importance of durability, maintenance, and flexibility in selecting wall art for vacation homes. Learn how to strike a balance between aesthetics and practicality, ensuring that the chosen decor withstands the wear and tear of regular guest turnover.

Art on a Dime: Budget-Friendly Wall Art Solutions for Property Enhancement

The Power of Affordable Elegance

Welcome to "Art on a Dime," where we unravel the secrets of enhancing your property without breaking the bank. In this guide, we'll explore budget-friendly wall art solutions that add elegance, style, and a touch of personality to your home. Say goodbye to the misconception that stunning wall decor comes with a hefty price tag. Join us on this journey to discover how creativity, resourcefulness, and a modest budget can transform your living spaces.

"Thrifty Treasures: Unveiling Hidden Gems in Secondhand Art"

In "Thrifty Treasures," we dive into the world of secondhand art, exploring thrift stores, flea markets, and online platforms to uncover hidden gems that won't break the bank. From vintage paintings to unique sculptures, learn the art of finding affordable treasures that add character and charm to your home. Discover the joy of the hunt and the satisfaction of bringing home one-of-a-kind pieces that elevate your space without denting your wallet.

Thrifty Treasures isn't just about saving money; it's about the thrill of discovering unique pieces that tell a story. Unlock the secrets of secondhand shopping and turn your budget-friendly finds into standout features in your home.

"DIY Delights: Crafting Personalized Wall Art on a Budget"

In "DIY Delights," we unleash the artist within and explore the world of do-it-yourself wall art projects. From simple canvas paintings to upcycled materials, discover how crafting your own wall decor allows you to personalize your space and stay within budget. Get inspired by easy-to-follow tutorials and step-by-step guides that turn everyday items into stunning pieces of art. Learn the art of self-expression through creativity, all while saving a considerable amount on your home enhancement journey.

DIY Delights isn't just about saving money; it's about infusing your home with a personal touch that reflects your unique style. Dive into the world of DIY and discover the satisfaction of creating wall art that is as individual as you are.

"Prints and Posters: Affordable Art That Packs a Punch"

In "Prints and Posters," we explore the vast world of affordable art prints that offer a cost-effective way to transform your walls. From classic posters to digital prints, understand how curated collections can bring cohesion and style to your living spaces. Discover the art of framing and arranging prints to create gallery-worthy displays that make a big impact without a big price tag. Say goodbye to bare walls and hello to an array of affordable prints that elevate your home.

Prints and Posters isn't just about affordability; it's about making strategic choices that create a visually stunning environment. Dive into the world of print curation and turn your space into a gallery of affordable yet impactful art.

"Nature's Bounty: Bringing the Outdoors In with Botanical Art"

In "Nature's Bounty," we turn to the beauty of the outdoors for inspiration, exploring the world of botanical art on a budget. From pressed flowers to botanical prints, learn how to infuse your space with the calming and refreshing elements of nature without splurging on expensive artworks. Dive into the versatility of botanical art and discover how it effortlessly complements various design styles, bringing a touch of the natural world into your home.

Nature's Bounty isn't just about affordability; it's about harnessing the beauty of nature to enhance your living spaces. Uncover the secrets of incorporating botanical art into your home and creating a tranquil haven that won't break the bank.

"Gallery Wall Magic: Maximizing Impact with a Mini Art Exhibition"

In "Gallery Wall Magic," we explore the strategy of creating a gallery wall to maximize the impact of your wall art. Learn the art of arranging and framing smaller pieces to create a mini art exhibition that draws the eye and adds visual interest to your space. Discover how to mix and match different styles, sizes, and frames to create a gallery wall that feels curated, intentional, and budget-friendly. Say goodbye to empty walls and hello to a dynamic display that showcases your style.

Gallery Wall Magic isn't just about affordability; it's about using strategic design to turn a collection of small pieces into a cohesive and impactful feature. Dive into the world of gallery walls and unlock the potential of your budget-friendly art collection.

"Art Swap: Trading Creativity for Affordable Wall Enhancements"

In "Art Swap," we explore the innovative concept of trading art with fellow enthusiasts to refresh your space without spending a dime. Learn the art of networking within creative communities, both online and offline, to exchange artworks and discover pieces that resonate with your taste. Dive into the collaborative spirit of art swapping and witness how this budget-friendly approach allows you to continually update your wall art collection with minimal financial investment.

Art Swap isn't just about saving money; it's about building connections and fostering a sense of community through the shared love of art. Embark on the journey of art swapping and experience the joy of finding new pieces to adorn your walls without spending a penny.

Cohesive Themes: Creating a Unified Look for Higher Property Value

Crafting Harmony - The Art of Cohesive Themes

Embark on a captivating exploration of how "Cohesive Themes" can elevate your property's allure and market value. Uncover the secrets of creating a harmonious aesthetic throughout your space, fostering a sense of unity that captivates potential buyers and enhances your property's overall appeal.

"The Power of First Impressions: Setting the Tone"

In "The Power of First Impressions," we delve into the crucial role of a unified theme in setting the tone for potential buyers. Learn how a cohesive exterior design, including landscaping and architectural elements, creates an immediate visual impact, drawing prospective homeowners into a world of curated beauty.

"Indoor Symphony: Cohesive Interior Design"

Explore "Indoor Symphony" as we navigate the intricacies of creating a harmonious interior. Discover how a consistent theme, whether it be minimalist, eclectic, or classic, ties together various rooms, providing a seamless flow that appeals to the emotions and aesthetics of potential buyers.

"The Garden Ensemble: Landscaping for Cohesion"

In "The Garden Ensemble," we uncover the importance of extending cohesive themes to outdoor spaces. Explore how thoughtfully designed landscaping, including gardens, patios, and outdoor structures, enhances the overall property value by offering a complete and unified experience.

"Color Palette Mastery: Weaving a Visual Thread"

Dive into "Color Palette Mastery" and learn the art of selecting and applying a unified color scheme. Understand how a well-chosen palette can tie together diverse elements, creating a visual thread that runs through each room and outdoor space, enhancing the property's aesthetic appeal.

"The Functional Elegance: Cohesive Themes and Practical Design"

In "The Functional Elegance," discover the delicate balance between aesthetics and practicality. Explore how cohesive themes can be seamlessly integrated with functional design, enhancing the property's usability, and further enticing potential buyers.

"Market Impact: The Appreciation of Cohesive Properties"

Conclude our journey with "Market Impact," where we discuss the tangible effects of cohesive themes on property appreciation. Understand how a unified look not only attracts buyers but also positions your property as a well-maintained, aesthetically pleasing investment that stands out in a competitive real estate market.

Staging Success: The Artful Guide to Transformative Home Presentation

The Art of First Impressions

Welcome to "Staging Success," where we unravel the secrets of using wall art to elevate the impact of home staging. In this guide, we'll explore the transformative power of art in making a lasting impression, turning potential buyers into enchanted admirers. Join us on this journey to discover how the strategic placement of wall art can redefine spaces, creating an atmosphere that resonates with buyers and leaves a memorable mark on their minds.

The Canvas of Potential - Setting the Stage for Success

In "The Canvas of Potential," we explore the foundational aspects of home staging and how art serves as the cornerstone for a successful presentation. Learn how to evaluate the unique characteristics of each room, considering factors such as size, lighting, and layout, to determine the most suitable art pieces. Discover the art of selecting wall art that complements the existing architecture and style of the home, creating a seamless transition that enhances rather than distracts.

Staging is not just about making a space look pretty; it's about telling a compelling story. The right selection of wall art sets the tone for this narrative, creating a visual language that resonates with potential buyers. By understanding the canvas of potential within each room, you can strategically utilize art to accentuate the positive features of the home, making it more appealing and memorable.

Art Styles and Home Harmony - Crafting Cohesive Spaces

Delve into "Art Styles and Home Harmony," where we explore how different art styles contribute to the overall cohesion of staged spaces. From modern minimalism to classic elegance, this section guides you through the process of selecting art that aligns with the existing decor while injecting a touch of personality. Discover the nuances of balancing various art styles to create a harmonious atmosphere that captivates buyers and allows them to envision the lifestyle the home offers.

Art should not compete with the space it is in; it should enhance it. By understanding the synergy between different art styles and existing decor, you can create a visual experience that feels curated and intentional. Whether it is abstract expressionism or timeless classics, the art you choose should contribute to the overall harmony of the home, creating an inviting and cohesive environment that appeals to a broad range of potential buyers.

Color Palette Mastery – Infusing Life and Energy

In "Color Palette Mastery," we explore the impact of color in home staging and how art becomes a powerful tool for infusing life and energy into spaces. This section guides you through the psychology of colors, helping you understand how different hues evoke emotions and influence perceptions. Learn to leverage the transformative power of color to create focal points, define spaces, and enhance the overall aesthetic appeal of the home.

Colors are not just visually pleasing; they are emotionally evocative. By mastering the art of color palettes, you can create a staged home that feels vibrant, welcoming, and emotionally resonant. From calming neutrals to bold statements, the right combination of colors in wall art can turn a house into a home, leaving potential buyers with a lasting impression of warmth and visual delight.

Strategic Placement - Guiding the Buyer's Eye

Embark on "Strategic Placement," where we unravel the importance of guiding the buyer's eye through the artful arrangement of wall pieces. This section provides insights into creating focal points, enhancing architectural features, and utilizing art to define the functionality of different spaces. Discover the subtle art of arranging art, ensuring that every piece contributes to the overall flow of the home and directs the buyer's attention to its most appealing aspects.

Art is not just about what you hang but also where you hang it. Strategic placement can transform a room, drawing attention to its strengths while downplaying any potential weaknesses. By guiding the buyer's eye, you can create a curated journey through the home, allowing them to appreciate each space and envision how they would inhabit and personalize it.

Scale and Proportion - Balancing Impact and Subtlety

Explore "Scale and Proportion," where we delve into the importance of balancing the impact of wall art with the subtlety required for effective staging. This section provides practical tips for selecting art pieces that complement the scale and proportion of each room, ensuring that they enhance rather than overwhelm the space. Discover how to strike the perfect balance, allowing potential buyers to appreciate the art without losing sight of the overall appeal of the home.

Size matters in the world of home staging. Oversized or undersized art can disrupt the visual harmony you're striving to achieve. By understanding the principles of scale and proportion, you can select art that fits seamlessly into each room, contributing to the overall aesthetic while maintaining a sense of balance and proportion that enhances the appeal of the space.

The Artful Finale - Leaving a Lasting Impression

Conclude our guide with "The Artful Finale," where we explore the finishing touches that solidify the impact of wall art in home staging. From creating memorable entryways to incorporating personalized touches, this section provides insights into the final details that leave a lasting impression on potential buyers. Discover the art of transforming a staged home into a memorable experience, ensuring that it remains etched in the minds of those who walk through its artfully adorned spaces.

Staging is not just about selling a property; it's about selling a lifestyle. The artful finale ensures that every potential buyer leaves with a sense of connection and a desire to make the staged home their own. By paying attention to the smallest details, you can create a lasting impression that sets your staged property apart from the rest, making it the memorable choice for buyers seeking a home that goes beyond bricks and mortar.

Art for All: The Rise of Affordable Elegance with Print on Demand

Welcome to a world where the walls of your home can be adorned with elegance without breaking the bank. In this blog post, we'll unravel the magic of print on demand art – a revolutionary concept that has made high-quality, sophisticated art accessible to everyone. From the affordability that doesn't compromise on quality to the vast array of artistic choices, join us on a journey into the realm of affordable elegance that print on demand brings to the art-loving community.

Affordable Elegance in Print on Demand Art:

Gone are the days when the words "affordable" and "elegant" were mutually exclusive in the world of art. Print on demand has emerged as a game-changer, making high-quality art accessible to all. This innovative approach allows artists to offer their creations in a cost-effective way, bringing the beauty of elegant artwork within reach for individuals who appreciate the finer things in life but may not have a millionaire's budget.

The affordability of print on demand art doesn't mean compromising on quality. With advancements in printing technology, artists can now reproduce their work with stunning precision and detail. From canvas prints that mimic the texture of an original painting to high-quality paper prints that capture the nuance of fine details, print on demand ensures that every art lover can adorn their space with pieces that exude elegance without the hefty price tag.

The Artistic Revolution: High-Quality Art Accessible through Print on Demand:

Print on demand has sparked an artistic revolution, democratizing the world of high-quality art. Traditional art acquisition often involves hefty investments, exclusive galleries, and limited choices. However, with print on demand, the art world opens its doors wide. Talented artists from around the globe can showcase their work without the constraints of traditional art markets, and art enthusiasts can explore a vast array of styles and themes from the comfort of their homes.

This revolution is not just about accessibility; it's about diversity. Print on demand platforms feature an eclectic mix of artistic expressions – from classic paintings and contemporary illustrations to abstract wonders and niche genres. The democratization of art means that everyone can find something that resonates with their taste, allowing them to curate a personal art collection that reflects their individuality.

Print on Demand Making Art Affordable and Elegant:

The marriage of affordability and elegance in print on demand art is a testament to the evolving landscape of the art market. Artists no longer need to compromise their vision to cater to a specific demographic; instead, they can create with authenticity while making their art accessible to a broader audience. The result is a win-win scenario where both artists and art enthusiasts benefit from a symbiotic relationship.

Print on demand platforms operate on a model that prioritizes efficiency. By eliminating the need for bulk production and excessive inventory, costs are reduced, allowing artists to price their work more affordably. This affordability doesn't translate to a compromise in quality; rather, it signifies a shift in the paradigm, where elegance is no longer reserved for the elite but is a privilege extended to all who appreciate the beauty of art.

The Canvas of Choice: Exploring Artistic Diversity in Print on Demand:

One of the unique strengths of print on demand lies in its ability to cater to diverse artistic tastes. Whether you're a fan of bold and vibrant colors, minimalist designs, or intricate details, print on demand platforms offer a canvas of choice that caters to every preference. The vast range of options ensures that your walls can reflect your personality, allowing you to create a space that feels uniquely yours.

Print on demand allows you to explore different mediums, styles, and artistic interpretations. From canvas prints that add texture to your space to framed prints that exude a polished elegance, the choices are as diverse as the artists contributing to these platforms. It is an invitation to step into a world of artistic diversity, where your walls can become a reflection of your eclectic taste and appreciation for the beauty that art brings to your life.

Beyond the Frame: Personalized Touches and Customization:

Print on demand not only brings affordability and elegance but also adds a layer of personalization to the art-buying experience. Many platforms allow you to customize your chosen artwork – from selecting the size of the print to choosing the type of framing or even tweaking the color palette. This level of personalization ensures that the art you bring into your home is not just a piece on the wall but a reflection of your unique taste and style.

Consider the joy of having a favorite quote overlaid on a serene landscape or a cherished family photo transformed into a gallery-worthy piece. Print on demand's commitment to customization allows you to infuse your personal touch into the art you choose, turning each piece into a conversation starter and a symbol of the stories that make your home uniquely yours.

The Future of Art: Print on Demand as a Catalyst for Change:

As we stand at the crossroads of affordability and elegance in art, print on demand emerges as a catalyst for change in the industry. This innovative approach has not only transformed how we acquire art but has also redefined the relationship between artists and their audience. It's a glimpse into the future where art is not confined to elite circles but is a shared experience, a collective celebration of creativity and expression.

The future of art with print on demand is a landscape where artists have the freedom to create authentically, where art enthusiasts can explore without financial barriers, and where the walls of our homes become vibrant canvases that tell stories, evoke emotions, and spark conversations. The democratization of art through print on demand is not just a trend; it's a shift in paradigm that heralds a more inclusive, diverse, and accessible era for the world of art.

Conclusion:

In the grand tapestry of art, print on demand has woven a thread of accessibility, affordability, and elegance. The walls of your home can now be adorned with pieces that tell stories, stir emotions, and reflect your unique taste, all without draining your wallet. As print on demand continues to reshape the landscape of the art world, we find ourselves at the forefront of a revolution where art is no longer a privilege but a shared joy for everyone to embrace.

Art in Unexpected Places: Surprising Spots to Boost Property Worth

Unlocking Hidden Potential with Artful Surprises

In a world where innovation meets aesthetics, "Art in Unexpected Places" unveils the hidden potential of your property. Join us on a journey through surprising spots where art can not only surprise but significantly enhance your property's overall worth.

"Elevating Nooks and Crannies: Transformative Art in Small Spaces"

Discover the magic of small spaces in "Elevating Nooks and Crannies." From underutilized corners to compact alcoves, explore how art can transform these overlooked areas into captivating focal points. Unearth the potential of sculptures, mini-installations, or even digital art displays to breathe life into spaces you might have dismissed.

"Artful Staircases: Ascending the Aesthetic Ladder"

In "Artful Staircases," we take a step-by-step approach to transforming often-neglected staircases into breathtaking features. Explore the possibilities of turning each step into a canvas, with murals, artistic railings, or strategically placed sculptures. Understand how the vertical flow of a staircase provides a unique storytelling opportunity.

"Artistic Storage: Beyond Functionality

to Aesthetic Appeal"

Dive into the world of "Artistic Storage," where functionality meets aesthetics. Uncover the potential of turning storage spaces into artistic marvels. From creatively designed cabinets to customized shelving showcasing curated art pieces, discover how mundane storage areas can become surprising highlights that add value to your property.

"Functional Art in Kitchens and Bathrooms: Aesthetic Utility"

"Functional Art" explores the unexpected marriage of utility and aesthetics in kitchens and bathrooms. Delve into the transformative power of art in spaces typically associated with functionality. Learn how to infuse creativity into everyday spaces, turning kitchens into culinary galleries and bathrooms into serene sanctuaries, enhancing your property's overall appeal.

"Artful Landscaping: Beyond the Garden, Beneath the Trees"

Experience the outdoors like never before in "Artful Landscaping." Shift your focus beyond traditional garden art and explore surprising spots beneath trees, within hedges, or along pathways. Understand how sculptures, hidden art installations, or even illuminated features can add an enchanting touch, turning your outdoor space into a masterpiece.

"The Art of Lighting: Illuminating Value in Unexpected Places"

Conclude our journey with "The Art of Lighting," where we shed light on the transformative power of illuminating unexpected spots. From hidden alcoves to overlooked architectural details, discover how strategic lighting paired with artistic elements can create stunning visual effects, adding both surprise and value to your property.

Choosing the Right Wall Art to Boost Your Home's Resale Value

The Art of Home Enhancement

Welcome to the world where art meets real estate in our guide on "Choosing the Right Wall Art to Boost Your Home's Resale Value." In this delightful exploration, we'll unravel the secrets of selecting the perfect wall art to not only elevate your living space but also significantly enhance the resale value of your home. From the entrance to the bedroom, discover how strategic art choices can turn your house into a buyer's dream.

The Grand Entrance - Setting the Tone

Step into "The Grand Entrance," where we explore the transformative power of the first impression. This section delves into the impact of foyer and hallway art on setting the tone for the entire home. Discover how a well-placed piece of art can immediately captivate potential buyers, creating a welcoming atmosphere that lingers in their minds throughout the tour.

Investing in the grand entrance isn't just about making a statement; it's about establishing a narrative for your home. By choosing wall art that reflects the overall vibe you want to convey, you not only make a lasting first impression but also guide buyers into envisioning the lifestyle your home offers.

Living Room Revelations – Creating a Centerpiece

Embark on "Living Room Revelations," where we uncover the central role of wall art in the heart of every home. This section explores how the right living room art can function as a visual centerpiece, anchoring the design and influencing the overall perception of the space. Dive into the nuances of selecting art that complements the room's style while appealing to a broad range of tastes.

The transformative power of living room revelations lies in its ability to turn a functional space into a showcase of lifestyle. By carefully curating art for your living room, you not only enhance the aesthetics for your own enjoyment but also create a focal point that resonates with potential buyers, elevating the perceived value of the entire home.

Kitchen Canvas - Infusing Style into Functionality

Step into "Kitchen Canvas," where we explore the often-overlooked potential of wall art in the heart of every home. This section delves into the art of infusing style into functionality, turning the kitchen into a vibrant space that goes beyond mere cooking. Discover how well-chosen art can contribute to a cohesive design, making the kitchen a memorable and aesthetically pleasing part of the home.

The transformative power of kitchen canvas lies in its ability to enhance the overall flow of the home. By selecting art that complements the kitchen's color scheme and style, homeowners can create a seamless transition between spaces, contributing to a unified design that adds to the property's appeal and resale value.

Bedroom Bliss - Creating a Relaxing Retreat

Embark on "Bedroom Bliss," where we delve into the impact of wall art on creating a relaxing retreat in the bedroom. This section explores the psychology behind bedroom art choices, focusing on creating a serene and personalized space that resonates with potential buyers. Discover how the right art can transform a bedroom into a sanctuary, showcasing the lifestyle possibilities your home offers.

The transformative power of bedroom bliss lies in its ability to convey a sense of comfort and luxury. By choosing art that enhances the bedroom's ambiance, homeowners not only improve their own quality of life but also appeal to buyers seeking a tranquil haven, ultimately influencing the perceived value of the entire property.

Bathroom Beautification – Elevating Everyday Spaces

Explore "Bathroom Beautification," where we discuss the often-under-estimated potential of wall art in the bathroom. This section delves into the art of elevating everyday spaces, turning bathrooms into visually appealing areas that contribute to the overall charm of the home. Discover how strategic art choices can create a spa-like atmosphere, leaving a positive and lasting impression on potential buyers.

The transformative power of bathroom beautification lies in its ability to showcase attention to detail and care in home maintenance. By selecting art that enhances the bathroom's aesthetic, homeowners can communicate a sense of pride in their property, positively impacting the perceived value and leaving a lasting impression on potential buyers.

Outdoor Oasis - Extending the Artistic Touch

Conclude our exploration with "Outdoor Oasis," where we uncover the impact of extending the artistic touch beyond the interior. This section delves into the transformative power of outdoor art, such as sculptures, murals, and decorative pieces, in creating an inviting exterior. Discover how a well-curated outdoor space can significantly enhance the curb appeal and overall value of your home.

The transformative power of outdoor oasis lies in its ability to create a seamless transition between indoor and outdoor living. By incorporating art into the outdoor spaces, homeowners not only enhance their own enjoyment but also make a bold statement to potential buyers, signaling that every corner of the property is carefully considered and inviting.

From The Purple House: Your Source for Stunning Art Prints

Are you looking to add a touch of elegance and sophistication to your home or office space? Look no further than FromThePurpleHouse, your go-to online website for finding stunning art prints.

We specialize in promoting print-on-demand art prints with a wide range of themes and styles, including abstract, contemporary, and modern. Our curated collection is designed to cater to the tastes of men and women aged 25 and older in the US and Canada who appreciate the beauty of art.

Art has the power to transform any space and evoke emotions. It can be a reflection of your personality and style, and at FromThePurpleHouse, we understand the importance of finding the perfect piece to enhance your decor and express your unique taste. That's why we offer a carefully selected collection of high-quality art prints on our Pictorem site that are sure to impress. Whether you're looking for a bold and vibrant abstract piece to make a statement, a contemporary print to add a modern touch, or a minimalist design to create a sense of calm, we have something for everyone.

Pictorems prints are created using the latest printing technology, ensuring that every detail is captured with precision and clarity. The colors are vibrant and true to life, making our prints a true work of art. One of the advantages of print-on-demand art prints is that they are customizable. You can choose the size, frame, and even the type of paper to suit your preferences and the specific needs of your space. This allows you to create a truly personalized piece that fits perfectly into your home or office.

At FromThePurpleHouse, we believe that art should be accessible to everyone. That's why we offer you competitive prices without compromising on quality. We work with talented artists from around the world to bring you a diverse range of styles and themes, ensuring that there is something for every taste and budget.

Shopping for art prints online can sometimes be overwhelming, but our user-friendly website makes it easy to browse and find the perfect piece. You can search by theme, style, or even color, making it convenient to narrow down your options and find exactly what you're looking for.

Our detailed product descriptions and high-resolution images on the Pictorem site give you a clear idea of what to expect, so you can make an informed decision. So why wait? Bring art into your life and transform your space with FromThePurpleHouse.

Shop our collection of stunning art prints today and discover the perfect piece to enhance your decor and express your unique style. With our high-quality prints and affordable prices, you can create a beautiful and inspiring space that you'll love coming home to.

https://www.pictorem.com/profile/Jodi.DiLiberto.

Mastering the Art of Investment: A Colorful Guide to Art Investment

Art is not just a feast for the eyes; it can be a savvy addition to your investment portfolio. In this guide, we'll embark on a journey through the intricacies of art investment, exploring the brushstrokes of financial growth and the vibrant world where aesthetics meet profit. So, grab your palette, and let's paint a picture of how art can be more than a passion—it can be a prudent investment strategy.

The Canvas of Potential: Understanding Art as an Investment

The first stroke on our canvas of art investment is understanding the potential behind this unique asset class. Unlike traditional investments, art has the power to appreciate both aesthetically and financially. While the art market can be influenced by trends, the value of certain artworks can soar over time, making it a dynamic and rewarding venture. Art investment allows you to diversify your portfolio, adding a touch of creativity to the world of finance. Navigating the art market requires a discerning eye. It's not just about buying what you love; it's about identifying artists with potential for future value appreciation. Research plays a pivotal role; staying informed about emerging artists, auction results, and market trends is key. By understanding the dynamics of the art world, you can position yourself to make informed investment decisions that go beyond personal taste.

The Brushstrokes of Research: Unveiling the Artist and the Market

In this section, we delve deeper into the importance of thorough research when considering art as an investment. Just as an artist meticulously plans each brushstroke, investors must navigate the canvas of information. Start by researching the artist—consider their reputation, exhibition history, and critical acclaim. A strong artist profile often translates into increased demand for their work, potentially boosting the value of your investment.

Understanding the broader art market is equally crucial. Auction results, gallery sales, and overall market trends provide valuable insights. Keep an eye on global art hubs, as different regions may have varying market dynamics. Additionally, exploring the history of an artwork, including provenance and exhibition history, can shed light on its journey and contribute to its overall value. Think of research as the foundation that supports the entire structure of your art investment strategy.

Palette of Potential: Investing in Emerging Artists

Venturing into the world of emerging artists is like discovering hidden treasures on the canvas of art investment. Emerging artists often offer a unique opportunity for growth as their works are relatively affordable compared to established names. Keep a keen eye on art schools, local galleries, and emerging talent showcases. These platforms are fertile ground for finding artists whose careers may be on the brink of blossoming.

Investing in emerging artists requires a blend of intuition and analysis. Look for artists with a distinct voice, a cohesive body of work, and potential for future recognition. Building relationships with artists and attending local exhibitions can provide a firsthand look at emerging trends and talents. While investing in emerging artists involves higher risk, it can also yield substantial returns as their careers flourish.

Auction Dynamics: Navigating the Hammer and Bids

Auctions are the heartbeat of the art market, pulsating with excitement and opportunity. Understanding the dynamics of art auctions is crucial for any art investor. The auction process is an intricate dance of bids, competition, and strategy. Familiarize yourself with auction houses, their reputations, and the types of artworks they specialize in. The auction setting can amplify the value of certain works through competitive bidding, creating a dynamic environment for potential returns.

Participating in auctions requires strategic thinking. Set a budget, do your pre-auction research, and be prepared to act decisively. Bidding strategically, whether online or in person, involves a delicate balance between assertiveness and restraint. By understanding auction dynamics, you can navigate the hammer's fall with confidence, securing artworks that align with your investment goals.

Preservation and Appreciation: Caring for Your Art Investment

Just as a masterpiece requires proper care to maintain its allure, your art investment demands thoughtful preservation. This section explores the importance of maintaining artworks to ensure their longevity and, subsequently, their financial value. Proper storage, climate control, and insurance are essential aspects of art investment. Whether you're a seasoned collector or a novice investor, understanding the art of preservation safeguards your investment against deterioration and damage.

Consider consulting conservation professionals to assess and address any potential issues with your artworks. Preservation efforts not only protect the physical condition of the art but also contribute to its overall provenance and authenticity. By investing in the long-term care of your collection, you enhance its potential for appreciation and maintain its allure for future generations.

Selling Strategies: Harvesting the Fruits of Your Art Investment

The final strokes on our canvas of art investment involve knowing when and how to harvest the fruits of your labor. Selling strategies play a pivotal role in realizing the financial gains from your art collection. Timing is key, and understanding market trends and demand fluctuations can influence the decision to sell. Keep an eye on the broader economic climate, as the art market is not immune to global financial shifts.

Explore various selling avenues, from private sales to auctions, and determine the approach that aligns with your goals. Building relationships with art dealers and galleries can open doors to potential buyers. Consider leveraging online platforms to reach a broader audience. Selling strategies should be informed by a combination of market analysis, financial goals, and a keen understanding of your collection's unique strengths.

Mastering the Art of Investment: A Colorful Guide to Art Investment

Art is not just a feast for the eyes; it can be a savvy addition to your investment portfolio. In this guide, we'll embark on a journey through the intricacies of art investment, exploring the brushstrokes of financial growth and the vibrant world where aesthetics meet profit. So, grab your palette, and let's paint a picture of how art can be more than a passion—it can be a prudent investment strategy.

Section 1: The Canvas of Potential: Understanding Art as an Investment

The first stroke on our canvas of art investment is understanding the potential behind this unique asset class. Unlike traditional investments, art has the power to appreciate both aesthetically and financially. While the art market can be influenced by trends, the value of certain artworks can soar over time, making it a dynamic and rewarding venture. Art investment allows you to diversify your portfolio, adding a touch of creativity to the world of finance. Navigating the art market requires a discerning eye. It's not just about buying what you love; it's about identifying artists with potential for future value appreciation. Research plays a pivotal role; staying informed about emerging artists, auction results, and market trends is key. By understanding the dynamics of the art world, you can position yourself to make informed investment decisions that go beyond personal taste.

Section 2: The Brushstrokes of Research: Unveiling the Artist and the Market

In this section, we delve deeper into the importance of thorough research when considering art as an investment. Just as an artist meticulously plans each brushstroke, investors must navigate the canvas of information. Start by researching the artist—consider their reputation, exhibition history, and critical acclaim. A strong artist profile often translates into increased demand for their work, potentially boosting the value of your investment.

Understanding the broader art market is equally crucial. Auction results, gallery sales, and overall market trends provide valuable insights. Keep an eye on global art hubs, as different regions may have varying market dynamics. Additionally, exploring the history of an artwork, including provenance and exhibition history, can shed light on its journey and contribute to its overall value. Think of research as the foundation that supports the entire structure of your art investment strategy.

Section 3: Palette of Potential: Investing in Emerging Artists

Venturing into the world of emerging artists is like discovering hidden treasures on the canvas of art investment. Emerging artists often offer a unique opportunity for growth as their works are relatively affordable compared to established names. Keep a keen eye on art schools, local galleries, and emerging talent showcases. These platforms are fertile ground for finding artists whose careers may be on the brink of blossoming.

Investing in emerging artists requires a blend of intuition and analysis. Look for artists with a distinct voice, a cohesive body of work, and potential for future recognition. Building relationships with artists and attending local exhibitions can provide a firsthand look at emerging trends and talents. While investing in emerging artists involves higher risk, it can also yield substantial returns as their careers flourish.

Section 4: Auction Dynamics: Navigating the Hammer and Bids

Auctions are the heartbeat of the art market, pulsating with excitement and opportunity. Understanding the dynamics of art auctions is crucial for any art investor. The auction process is an intricate dance of bids, competition, and strategy. Familiarize yourself with auction houses, their reputations, and the types of artworks they specialize in. The auction setting can amplify the value of certain works through competitive bidding, creating a dynamic environment for potential returns.

Participating in auctions requires strategic thinking. Set a budget, do your pre-auction research, and be prepared to act decisively. Bidding strategically, whether online or in person, involves a delicate balance between assertiveness and restraint. By understanding auction dynamics, you can navigate the hammer's fall with confidence, securing artworks that align with your investment goals.

Section 5: Preservation and Appreciation: Caring for Your Art Investment

Just as a masterpiece requires proper care to maintain its allure, your art investment demands thoughtful preservation. This section explores the importance of maintaining artworks to ensure their longevity and, subsequently, their financial value. Proper storage, climate control, and insurance are essential aspects of art investment. Whether you're a seasoned collector or a novice investor, understanding the art of preservation safeguards your investment against deterioration and damage.

Consider consulting conservation professionals to assess and address any potential issues with your artworks. Preservation efforts not only protect the physical condition of the art but also contribute to its overall provenance and authenticity. By investing in the long-term care of your collection, you enhance its potential for appreciation and maintain its allure for future generations.

Section 6: Selling Strategies: Harvesting the Fruits of Your Art Investment

The final strokes on our canvas of art investment involve knowing when and how to harvest the fruits of your labor. Selling strategies play a pivotal role in realizing the financial gains from your art collection. Timing is key, and understanding market trends and demand fluctuations can influence the decision to sell. Keep an eye on the broader economic climate, as the art market is not immune to global financial shifts.

Explore various selling avenues, from private sales to auctions, and determine the approach that aligns with your goals. Building relationships with art dealers and galleries can open doors to potential buyers. Consider leveraging online platforms to reach a broader audience. Selling strategies should be informed by a combination of market analysis, financial goals, and a keen understanding of your collection's unique strengths.

The Art of Thrifty Collecting: Budget-Friendly Tips for Building Your Art Collection

Embarking on an art collection journey doesn't have to break the bank. In this guide, we'll explore the world of budget-friendly art collecting, where creativity meets affordability. Discover how to curate a captivating art collection without draining your wallet. So, let's roll up our sleeves, put on our bargain-hunting hats, and delve into the exciting realm of thrifty art collecting.

Thrift Store Treasures: Unearthing Gems on a Shoestring Budget

Thrift stores are treasure troves waiting to be explored. This section dives into the thrill of discovering affordable art in unexpected places. From quaint paintings to quirky sculptures, thrift stores often harbor hidden gems that can become the crown jewels of your collection. The key is to approach thrift store hunting with an open mind—be ready to embrace the eclectic and find beauty in the unconventional.

Keep an eye out for frames that may outshine the artwork they hold. A little DIY magic can breathe new life into these pieces, transforming them into unique, personalized creations. Thrift store art hunting is not just about finding bargains; it's about the joy of the hunt, the serendipity of stumbling upon unexpected masterpieces that resonate with your taste and budget.

Local Talent Spotlight: Supporting Emerging Artists on a Budget

This section explores the exciting avenue of discovering and supporting local artists. Emerging talents often offer affordable pieces that not only fit your budget but also contribute to the growth of the artistic community. Attend local art fairs, community exhibitions, and open studios to connect with artists who are just beginning to make their mark. Purchasing directly from the artist ensures that your investment goes directly into the hands of those who pour their passion onto the canvas.

Consider collaborating with local art schools or community art programs. Student showcases and exhibitions can be goldmines for affordable, yet promising, pieces. Supporting local talent not only benefits your collection but fosters a sense of community, making your art collection a reflection of the vibrant creative energy in your area.

Online Adventures: Navigating Digital Platforms for Budget-Friendly Finds

The digital era opens up a world of possibilities for budget-friendly art collecting. Explore online platforms, auction websites, and social media to uncover affordable art that suits your taste. Websites like Etsy, eBay, and even Instagram connect buyers with artists globally, offering a diverse array of styles and mediums. Keep an eye on emerging trends and artists who gain traction online—they might be the next big thing in your collection.

Engage with online art communities and forums where collectors share tips and discoveries. Participate in online auctions, where bidding wars can sometimes lead to unexpected steals. The virtual realm isn't just a place to find affordable art; it's a dynamic space where the global art community converges, creating opportunities for budget-friendly collecting that transcends geographical boundaries.

DIY Masterpieces: Unleashing Your Inner Artist on a Dime

Channel your inner artist in this section, where we explore the budget-friendly world of DIY art. Creating your own masterpieces not only saves money but adds a personal touch to your collection. No need to be a professional artist—abstracts, collages, and mixed media projects can be both therapeutic and visually striking. Experiment with different mediums and let your creativity run wild. Consider hosting DIY art sessions with friends or joining community workshops. Embrace imperfection and let each piece tell a story. DIY art not only expands your collection affordably but also fosters a sense of accomplishment and personal connection with your artistic endeavors.

Framing Magic: Elevating Budget-Friendly Art with Stylish Frames

In this section, we'll explore how framing can transform budget-friendly art into gallery-worthy pieces. Invest in stylish frames that enhance the visual impact of your collection. Discount stores, thrift shops, and online retailers often offer a variety of affordable framing options. Choose frames that complement the artwork and add a touch of sophistication to your display.

Consider mixing and matching frames to create a dynamic gallery wall. Experiment with unconventional frames or repurpose vintage ones for added character. Framing is not just a functional aspect; it's an art in itself that can elevate the overall aesthetic of your collection without breaking the bank.

Smart Collecting: Nurturing Your Collection on a Budget

The final section of our budget-friendly art collecting guide delves into smart collecting practices. Patience is a virtue in the world of thrifty art collecting. Resist the urge for impulsive purchases and take the time to curate a collection that aligns with your taste and budget. Set a realistic budget for each piece and stick to it. Remember, the joy of budget-friendly collecting lies not only in the affordability but in the satisfaction of building a collection thoughtfully. Regularly reassess your collection and identify pieces that may no longer align with your evolving taste or investment goals. Consider swapping or selling these pieces to make room for new additions. Smart collecting involves a continuous process of curation and refinement, ensuring that your collection remains a reflection of your aesthetic journey.

Masterpieces and Mansions: Investing in Fine Art for Property Appreciation

Introduction: The Art of Wealth Accumulation

Welcome to a journey where canvas meets concrete, exploring the symbiotic relationship between "Masterpieces and Mansions." In this guide, we'll unravel the narrative of how investing in fine art can be a shrewd move for property appreciation. From gallery walls to home halls, discover how the strokes of a brush can elevate your estate and your financial portfolio.

Section 1: The Canvas Advantage - Adding Aesthetic Value

Dive into "The Canvas Advantage," where we uncover how investing in fine art transcends mere aesthetics. This section explores the transformative power of a well-curated art collection in enhancing the visual appeal of a property. Discover how carefully chosen artworks can turn a house into a home, creating a unique and memorable environment that captivates visitors and potential buyers alike.

Beyond the aesthetic enhancement, the canvas advantage lies in the ability

of fine art to convey a sense of sophistication and cultural refinement. When prospective buyers walk into a home adorned with exquisite art pieces, they aren't just entering a living space—they're stepping into a curated world that speaks volumes about taste and discernment. This aesthetic value becomes an intrinsic part of the property, setting it apart in the real estate market.

Section 2: Rarity as a Commodity - Investing in Limited Editions

Embark on "Rarity as a Commodity," where we explore the allure of limited editions in the world of fine art investment. This section delves into how owning exclusive pieces can add an element of rarity to your property, making it stand out in a sea of conventional homes. Discover the investment potential of limited-edition artworks and how their scarcity can drive appreciation both in the art market and the real estate realm.

The scarcity principle is a powerful force in the world of investment. Just as limited edition artworks become coveted treasures, properties adorned with such pieces gain a unique cachet. Potential buyers recognize the exclusivity, creating a perception of elevated value and desirability, factors that can significantly contribute to the appreciation of your real estate asset.

Section 3: Art as a Conversation Starter - Building Emotional Connections

Step into "Art as a Conversation Starter," where we explore the social and emotional aspects of fine art in a property. This section delves into how art can become a bridge for human connection, fostering positive emotions and memorable experiences. Discover the potential of art to create an emotional resonance with visitors and potential buyers, leaving a lasting impact that extends beyond the physical confines of the property.

Art has the incredible ability to evoke emotions, tell stories, and stimulate conversations. When strategically placed within a home, artworks become more than embellishments; they become catalysts for dialogue. A property with a captivating art collection becomes a space where memories are made, forging an emotional connection that lingers in the minds of those who experience it. This emotional resonance can significantly enhance the perceived value of the property.

Section 4: The Investment Spectrum - Balancing Risk and Reward

Explore "The Investment Spectrum," where we navigate the delicate balance between risk and reward in the world of fine art investment. This section delves into the potential financial gains of investing in art, considering factors such as market trends, artist reputation, and historical significance. Discover how a well-considered art investment strategy can contribute to the overall appreciation of your property portfolio.

Investing in fine art is not only an aesthetic endeavor but a strategic financial move. Art values can appreciate over time, sometimes outperforming traditional investment assets. By diversifying your investment portfolio to include art, you not only enrich the visual appeal of your property but also position yourself to benefit from the potential financial gains that a carefully curated art collection can bring.

Section 5: Showcasing Local Talent - Community Engagement

Embark on "Showcasing Local Talent," where we delve into the intersection of art investment and community engagement. This section explores the idea of supporting local artists and how it can enhance the value of your property. Discover the impact of fostering a vibrant local art scene on the overall appeal of your neighborhood and the potential to attract like-minded, culturally aware buyers.

Investing in fine art becomes a community-building effort when you choose to showcase local talent. By incorporating pieces from regional artists, you contribute to the cultural richness of your neighborhood. This engagement not only fosters a sense of pride among locals but also positions your property as a hub of creativity, attracting buyers who value community connections and artistic expression.

Section 6: Artful Legacy - Passing Down Aesthetic Wealth

Conclude our journey with "Artful Legacy," where we explore the concept of passing down aesthetic wealth through generations. This section delves into how a carefully curated art collection becomes a timeless legacy, enhancing the allure and value of a property for future owners. Discover the potential of creating a living, breathing masterpiece that transcends time and serves as a testament to your refined taste and investment foresight.

Investing in fine art isn't just about the present; it's about creating a legacy. A well-curated collection, passed down through generations, becomes an integral part of a property's identity. Future owners inherit not only the physical space but also the stories, emotions, and cultural significance embedded in the artworks. This enduring legacy adds a layer of timeless value to the property, making it a living testament to the confluence of art and real estate.

Acknowledgement

For **Jodi DiLiberto**— the artist whose vision colors my world.

Your creativity is a reminder that art is not just something we make, but something we *live*. Your courage, your curiosity, and the way you transform emotion into color continue to inspire every page I write.

To anyone holding this book: If you wish to see the heart behind my own creative life, visit Jodi's work at **From the Purple House: www.fromthepurplehouse.art**

Her art is a world of its own—vibrant, intuitive, and deeply human. I'm endlessly grateful to walk beside her.

About The Author

Neil J Milliner

Neil J. Milliner is a contemporary author, creative educator, and publisher focusing on helping creatives, introverts, and musicians build authentic brands, overcome perfectionism, and navigate career challenges through practical, psychology-backed guides. He writes books on music marketing (*The Musician's Marketing Playbook), songwriting (*Emotional Hooks Handbook), sustainable living, self-improvement (*How to Feel Better Without Fixing Everything), and building creative spaces. He runs his own imprint, Books by Neil J, and emphasizes connecting with one's core self for aligned, meaningful creation.

Key Themes in His Work:
- Authenticity: Building brands and creating music that reflects your true self.
- Overcoming Perfectionism: Practical strategies to move past creative blocks and endless tweaking.
- Music Industry Guidance: Marketing, songwriting, and technical advice for musicians.
- Mindful Living: Eco-habits and personal growth for creatives.

Who He Helps:
- Musicians, songwriters, producers
- Creative introverts
- Entrepreneurs and creatives seeking genuine connection
- Individuals wanting to live more sustainably